Old City,
New Rumours

Old City, New Rumours

Poems from Hull

Edited by
Ian Gregson
and Carol Rumens

Five Leaves Publications
www.fiveleaves.co.uk

Published with the assistance of
the Philip Larkin Society

Old City, New Rumours
Poems from Hull

Edited by Ian Gregson and Carol Rumens

Published in 2010 by
Five Leaves Publications,
PO Box 8786, Nottingham NG1 9AW
www.fiveleaves.co.uk

Published with the assistance of
the Philip Larkin Society
(www.philiplarkin.com)

ISBN: 978 1 905512 93 5

Five Leaves is a member of Inpress,
representing independent publishers
(www.inpressbooks.co.uk)

Cover image: James Booth

Design and typesetting:
Four Sheets Design and Print

Printed in Great Britain

Contents

Foreword by Carol Rumens

The thirty poets assembled in our anthology – eleven of them contributors to *A Rumoured City* (Ed. Douglas Dunn, Bloodaxe Books, 1982) – have a variety of associations with Hull. A few are natives, or from not far away; a few still live there, or not far away. Some are Hull University alumni or current staff-members; others, still more temporary visitors. As one of the poets born and raised in Hull, Maurice Rutherford, says, 'It matters not at all from where they came,/the pigeons or the poets; *poems* remain-/well, some...' ('The Hull Poets – and Pigeons,'). I believe we have gathered here a good many of those poems that, wherever their authors are from, deserve to remain.

We have not attempted to include every Hull poet. In any artistically lively place there will always be changes happening faster than they can be chronicled: a new movement or name may emerge even as the editors send off the last corrected proof of a book already become a little old-fashioned. This is inevitable – and thoroughly healthy. We trust that these newer – and older – poets of Hull will be honoured in other collections. As for our anthology, it seemed that to include fewer poets but to represent those who were included by more than one poem would be the worthiest use of our space.

Today's poets, needing to woo what is for many their new patrons, the universities, may become temporary residents of many cities during their lives. As one such wanderer, I have found the experiences rolled up in the standard parcel rich and educative. There are, however, places that the outsider senses as closed fists, despite the pleasant smiles. Others are fists that unclose a little way, but no further. Hull, though, has been, or appeared to be, an open hand. It is always important to find a community of the like-minded – other writers, of course, but, equally important, gifted scholars and fresh-thinking students. One arrives keenly receptive – but it is also vital to be received, and welcomed into the literary dialogue, however annoying one's ignorance of the customs and language may be. The creative-combative 'give-and-take-that' of a literary community within the university is not less important than a fascinatingly varied urban and industrial topography, a sense of historical continuity, a unique geography shaped by two differently-great rivers, and straight-talking, warm-hearted local people. These are what Hull has given me, besides the indefinable moods connected to a place once inhabited by possibly the greatest and most disturbing of 20th-century English poets. The poems in *Old City, New Rumours* testify to the stimuli many others have experienced. Mixed with a little imagination, and a sprinkling of the entirely unpredictable, such elements may begin to swirl around in a writer's personal poetry-alembic and produce glimmers of gold that would never have otherwise appeared, even if the place itself does not always appear in the finished product.

For me, co-editing this anthology also provides an opportunity to say 'Thank you, Hull: thank you, Hull University.'

Introduction by Ian Gregson

Philip Larkin is certainly a major reason why Hull has become a hotspot for poetry. He describes the city as 'unpretentious, recent, full of shops and special offers like a television commercial' – sounding close to his 'cut-price crowd' – but then notices that:

> Behind Hull is the plain of Holderness, lonelier and lonelier, and after that the birds and lights of Spurn Head, and then the sea. One can go ten years without seeing these things, yet they are always there, giving Hull the air of having its face half-turned towards distance and silence, and what lies beyond them.

That description evokes what it was in the landscape of Hull that aroused a feeling of affinity in Larkin, because the endings of his poems repeatedly open onto silent distances which form a dissolving transition into an inviting, but also disquieting, 'beyond'. It also strikes a note that poems about Hull have repeatedly struck, so that it becomes a Hull signature – that conviction that estuarial mud contains epiphanic hints of transcendence. Larkin's presence in the city drew others to it and made powerful members of the poetry world willing to become writers in residence at the University where he ran the library. More recently the University's Larkin Centre has institutionalised the formerly looser influence which he exerted, and given more definite shape and purpose to the willingness of poets to make pilgrimages to a city where such a distinctive poetic voice had spoken with increasing authority. Although an idea rather than a physical entity, since its inception in 2005 the Centre has been an important focus of the University's strong support for Creative Writing, the introduction of which into both undergraduate and postgraduate curricula has had several positive effects. It has meant an increasing number of enthusiastic professional writers joining the teaching staff. The various Larkin Centre directors, themselves writers, have each in turn ensured a steady flow of guest poets and novelists into the University to give informal MA seminars and public readings. Most significantly, there are signs now of a body of talented post-graduate creative writing students emerging. If Hull in the past has somehow failed to attract women poets in any considerable number, an absence clearly reflected in the pages of this anthology, the balance seems about to be rectified, with several promising women poets among the current MA cohort.

Larkin, on the other hand, was never interested in gathering young poets around him, which is the activity which makes certain places resonate as centres where poetry happens – the activity of Philip Hobsbaum in Belfast and Peter Sansom, in Huddersfield and, now, Sheffield. It was Douglas Dunn who performed this activity in Hull in the mid-1970s, though, again, this couldn't have happened without Larkin, who had spotted the talent of the young Scotsman early on. Douglas became a writer in residence, even though he was in residence already, but he worked at helping young poets above and beyond (and after) the duties of that role. He was astonishingly generous with his time and money; he was sustaining himself strenuously as a freelance writer but he allowed aspiring poets to go to his house and pester him with mostly hopeless poems. He took Tony Flynn, Tony Griffin and myself on a reading tour when what we had to read was almost entirely not worth hearing; we gave a reading in Scunthorpe where, because of a misprint, many in the audience were expecting pottery. *The Rumoured City* gave published form to the work that Douglas had done in helping poets living in Hull between 1974 and 1982 and helped to promote many of the poets it anthologised. Its 'Preface' by Larkin – from

11

which I quote above – indicates the godfatherly presence, behind all this activity, of the senior poet. And this anthology, *Old City, New Rumours* refers to its 1982 predecessor and follows its precedent of including both natives of Hull and poets who lived there later, mostly in roles related to the university.

Hull has benefited from the efforts of many people since Douglas's formative activities, but John Osborne has to be mentioned as pre-eminent amongst them. His work in *Bete Noire*, both the magazine and the readings, was enormously influential in the late 80s and 90s in broadcasting the literary impact of Hull. The energy which John bestowed on it bestowed widespread benefits both on writers connected to Hull and on the Hull literary scene. It must be said, however, that the *Bete Noire* years would not have happened without the earlier work which Douglas had performed a decade earlier and it's this which I'm most qualified to describe. *The Rumoured City* poets were never all together in one place – though there was one evening class where most of the men, at least, were present, and Sean O'Brien read a poem that started 'Your season, Norman'. When I recall the sound of bleak fretting in that poem, I'm aware that Sean was already inventing the rueful plangency that would make him famous. But the main thing I remember about Sean was that the dangling and distressed hem of his jeans scuffed along floors and pavements in a way that wasn't fashionable until decades later. Peter Didsbury's exotic influences included Christopher Middleton and John Ashbery, and he wrote poems of an enviable strangeness. He was never fully present in any company, as though half his mind was occupied with the Sumerian subjunctive, or whether or not he'd left his back door open. Sean and Peter were friends but they were very different from each other, both as people and as poets, and I think it's because of the diversity that was evident in *A Rumoured City* that poets who came after that period felt able to make their own distinctive contribution. *Old City, New Rumours* therefore expresses an even greater diversity because it represents a much greater period of time for poets connected to a city which, as Larkin wrote, helps poets because 'a place cannot produce poems: it can only not prevent them, and Hull is good at that.'

Three Poems by Peter Didsbury

A Fire Shared

This evening I have spent
in the Irishwoman's room.
A fire shared is a fire cheaper.

A twelvemonth since
I knew her not at all.
Our hearths were crowded then
but now it is fitting
that one of them bides cold.
A fire shared is a fire cheaper by far.

She has enough English now
for January tales
of our slavering *bargeist*,
which stalks these dark flagged yards
intent on the taking of children.
She would not have understood a year ago.

A year ago her English was just enough
for blessing or cursing,
to ask the price of bread
or directions to a pump.
But now a fire shared
is a fine instructive tutor.

She has enough English now
to match my *bargeists* and goblins
with *pookas* and suchlike,
and I find I have learned what these are,
from many a night
spent sharing and cheapening fire.

A twelvemonth ago I would not have known
the Irish for 'sorrow', 'cholera', 'children',
or who stood by me at the same wide grave-mouth
as we wept after each of our fashions.
But now I know these things,
which are things I have learned
in the school of the ruined hearth,
which is held in both our rooms,
where a fire shared
is the cheapest fire of all.

Owl and Miner

The owl alights on his shoulder.
All the day-shift she's waited patiently there,
high in the pine that grows hard-by the pit-head.
Waited blinking and dreaming,
and turning the slow escutcheon of her face.
Waited as that which would serve to draw her master
back with songs from his deep Plutonic shades.

Thus it is that he steps from the earth and is greeted.
She furls her wings, and as they set off
on their mile up the darkening lane,
towards the low-banked cloud of the clustering houses,
he starts to sing to her. I see his white smoke.
His breath on the air he casts as if he would net
the voices of ghosts in the empty elder trees.
For it is winter now, and his songs are of winter.
Wind unparcelled across the keen land.
First light snowfall turning black on hedge.
Warren and iron pool and far road-end,
where now the yellow lights begin to come on,
in twos and threes, haltingly, as if to conjure
the stars to commence their stammering nightly speech.

Coasts of Africa 1850

Deceased for many years was engaged in the
suppression of the African slave trade.
(OBITUARY OF WILLIAM HENRY HOBDAY,
FLEETWOOD CHRONICLE, JANUARY 1912).

Undo the thong that closes the mouth of the bag.
Spill William Hobday's coins upon the board.
Build from their falling and rocking into silence
the boom of sheets and blocks and the gasp
of a wind that carries the reek of the swamp in its hair.
Hear him sing of home.
Hear him tell the tale of the names of the coasts
on imagined bracelets of turquoise and citrine beads.
Hear him name the white forts.
Summon him now.
Then down in one the glass of yellow bile
that he brings to your side from the quarter deck
      to hand you.
Watch him carry a *nigger* up from a hold
to save her ulcerous feet from the salt-scoured planks.
Or stand and gaze with him through lidless eyes
at a barque a cable ahead as it jettisons *cargo*.
Summon him here by reciting in a loud voice
the poundage of cannon and shot.
Oh summon him here with the names of carronadoes,
with those of comrades, with canister and swivel.
Summon him here from *Philomel*, and that this might
      come to pass
consume in mind's flame his oak tobacco jar,
let flame devour his ribbons and his papers,
construct a pyre and arrange that all his pain
should tumble to ash, with the last of his books about God.
And let there be smoke. And let the smoke
roll out like mercy to bear the sailor home.
Let the smoke caress in the semblance of a breeze

17

that beach by the Irish Sea where he paddles at evening.
Then let the smoke vanish, except that it should lie
in the mouth of his jug as the froth upon the beer
he's just been out to fetch,
and now, soothed with stern psalms,
is carrying home in his old man's dappled hand.

Two Poems by Douglas Dunn

Ripe Bananas

After the dark morning, February blue
Shakes the dishevelled, lingering pods,
Resistant leaves, the mossed rose-tree.
Each day is longer now
By a few measurable minutes
Enough to contrive late afternoon
Or sun-over-the-yardarm.
Robins still roll through the cotoneasters
Or pose on the bird-feeder.
I notice how central heating protects
Surviving fruit flies. Ripe bananas
Show off their bruises. They'll last
Another day unless I eat them first
Or bake banana muffins.
A robin on a wheelbarrow puffs out its breast,
Show-off, and nasty with it.
As a member of the RSPB
I'm a bit disgusted by these bully robins.
A door shifts on a draught, a spider's lace
Moves on a puff that just might be my breath.
I can hear an oatcake crumble,
Tiny disturbances of dust and fluff,
Bubbles fizzing in
My Bombay-and-tonic,
This pencil on this paper.
Somehow, they're enough of noise
For a domestic symphony,
A solitude sufficiently robust
To encourage mumbles of wonder.

The House of the Blind

I

When you sat on the upper deck of the bus
You could see the white metal banisters
On the stepped pathways.

Once, on a winter's morning,
I saw someone being taught to climb steps.
The rail would have been cold and wet on his hands.

That Spring, a raincoated man in dark spectacles
Would have felt similarly cold and wet,
But been refreshed by the scent of lilacs.

On a summer's day, I saw a woman
Instructed in the use of her first guide-dog.
Even now the tug on her arms pulls at my heart.

I could be the last poet in the language
To say 'heart' in the traditional way.
I hope not. I'm writing about eyes.

After a catastrophe of spectacles,
This autumn I walk in a blur.
My daughter's nudge on my arm makes me think of that
    stranger.

II

The coffee was good. I was on my third cup.
From opened windows across the street
Instrumentalists were practising –

Flutes, clarinets, trumpets, violins, several pianos.
In lulls for tuition or advice, a fine soprano
Stopped people in their shoes, listening.

A cellist surrendered to Bach with a passion.
I could imagine the genderless sway,
Planing the air, ironing sound.

I felt so glad to be in Prague, and free,
With time on my hands, and *Turandot* in the evening.
An oboe lingered, in love with Mozart.

Several students emerged with cased instruments.
They unpocketed, then unfolded, their white sticks.
I think the waiter was watching for my reaction.

His smile was benign, but proud, and defiant.
All day, every day, he listens to their music.
His smile broadened, and he nodded,

Approving my look of sympathetic surprise;
And, after three shots of strong black coffee, my cup
Was the more tremblingly lifted up.

III

After Louis Braille accidentally put his eye out
With an awl in his father's workshop,
And the other eye sympathized with its dead partner,

A great kindness began in his darkness.
There was reading by raised dots before him,
Invented for French artillerymen to plan

The fall of shot in the dark without giveaway lamps.
The gunners couldn't read, not even in daylight.
Braille refined, perfected, and made it a useful thing.

21

Thomas Edison invented the gramophone
To provide speaking books for the blind.
Tin Pan Alley and the entire repertoire

Recorded from a foundation in benevolence!...
I've watched a blind student read a poem in Braille,
And then say it aloud, in perfect cadence,

Her voice delighting me. She's never seen
A poem, but she reads and hears. I write
To be read by eyes, and mind, and fingers.

IV

When you lose an eye, then you can lose the other,
Like Louis Braille, by 'sympathetic ophthalmia'
It doesn't happen often. But you lose a dimension

As my love discovered, hanging out the washing
On a line that felt uncertain, flat, and vague.
After that, I did it. Sympathy's mutual.

I hung the washing on a line that wavered.
That was as nothing to my love's nightmare –
Hanging washing on a line that wasn't there.

Three Poems by Andy Fletcher

the boating trip

i'm really enjoying the boating trip
when you point out we're not on water at all
but in the middle of a field

i look at
the grass around us
the soil stuck to the ends of the oars

i pull harder
until the rowlocks rattle and knock
until I hear the thud of waves at the bow
and spray comes over and dampens my shirt

still i row
until sweat rolls down my forehead into my eyes
until i can no longer see where we're going

the den

we didn't know
about pondichery or guadeloupe
we didn't know what 'fribbled' meant
though we fribbled about in our den
playing at buses
ding you were saying *ding ding*
we were unaware
of the north west direction of the wind
of the movement of molecules under bark
of a distant dome that was about to crack

with naked knees
we explored dark corners and moss
without understanding how bacteria
were multiplying on our sandwiches laid on a stone
without understanding the impact
of the second world war

gaps in the wall needed mud
a hole in the roof needed sticks

with no idea of my respiratory system i coughed
without being conscious of my facial muscles i laughed
we weren't concerned with eternity
the universe or god with failure or fear
only in how the sun found a way in
and made a small circle of light on the grass

meeting you

i go to the station to meet you

the train stops at the buffers
passengers with suitcases and bags get off

i look through the faces for yours

the next day
i go to the station to meet you

pigeons flap into the air as the train pulls in

people step off wave to relations
light cigarettes hug loved ones

every day
i go to the station to meet you
soon from the mass of faces
i know you'll appear and smile

years pass

the station's refurbished
old trains are replaced by new ones
timetables change

still i stand on the platform
litter blows towards me
plastic bags rise from the tracks

each day
i go to the station to meet you

Three Poems by Tony Flynn

The Gravity of Lovelessness

'Two forces rule the universe:
light and gravity.'
    SIMONE WEIL

Several tons of weightlessness
– a feather from the wing of God –

might counterweigh
what felt like gravity

inside her:-
in-

finitesimal, it
tips the scales, next

though it is to
nothingness, less

even than a
tiny breath,

which she would
weigh out in her heart

against the worst,
as Plato might have

once so weighed
the Good it-

self on
Ideal scales: love's

equilibrium, this
counterpoise,

should such a lightness
come to lift

all of what is
from the pull of itself,

'...and so in
plants by virtue of the sun's

energy caught up
by the green leaves

can matter find its way
upward

against the law of gravity –
The tree is really rooted in the sky.'

Seeing Voices

For Donna

Only with the light
on my lips can you
read what I would

say to you – sweet
nothings come
to nothing

in the dark, unless I
let my tongue
excite

its little code
along your spine – You
shiver at the word made flesh.

Body Language

Days when her stomach eats itself:
food she has pared to imagined morsels
– longing gorged on nothingness –

starves her body until it gives up
a self as thin as the "I" she writes
in such letters home as would

never be sent, each
little more than a famished
breath, which

tell how she's
almost managed it, almost
already disappeared,

like the legible
ghost or impression left
that haunts the blank sheet underneath.

Two Poems by Cliff Forshaw

Ned Kelly's Eyes
After Sidney Nolan

That's him, that awkward shadow, that black, that's Ned.
　　He's painted out as if already dead.

Sometimes, it's just a blank, that slit for eyes.
　　You look right through the man to clear blue skies.

Sometimes, that void's red-tinged with fire or dawn:
　　the burbling billy-can, the day's first yawn.

Sometimes, the clouds in that gash blush with dusk:
　　sky buries its burning cheek down in the dust.

Sometimes, there's a flash of silver, say sardines:
　　that peeled-back strip you've keyed along the tin.

He has no eyes in the back of his head, of course.
　　Sometimes, he rides away (*Black gun. Black horse.*)

into another picture. What's forged by smith
　　from black's still fire-lit then, and riding into myth.

Wake

very loosely after the Latin of Sextus Propertius IV. 7.
"Sunt aliquid manes. Letum non omnia finit"

i. The Visitation

Death's not the end of it, this much I know
– ghosts *do* exist – they walk right through our walls.
Can't keep them down under shovelled earth, the dead
watch us while we sleep, peep in at your window,
lean like a leprous moon over our beds.
I know this for a fact – and this is how:
I saw her, the other night, just after the funeral.
I woke and she was *there*, a pale shadow
inches from my face, almost sharing my pillow,
watching, just watching me. Her eyes burned blue,
like chips of electric ice; kohl eyeshadow.

Her skin had this weird unhealthy glow
(not surprising – we'd buried her that day).
Oh Christ – her bones shone through as if X-rayed.
I thought of some translucent, poisonous creature,
a fish – fluorescent, flattened by cold, dark pressure –
that flesh I'd loved trawled up from horrible depths.

No, death's not the end of it. Far from it. Death's
too good for us. Not good enough for them.
They go on, and on. Won't let us left behind
get any sleep until we finally wake
– shit-scared, sweat-wet and shivering – to find
it's your funeral now.
You're guest of honour at this other wake.
Fear in your throat, you solemnly swear,
under pain of god-knows-what torment, ache,
to set things right – or never sleep again.

31

She's got you bang on. You get described.
Her bony finger jabs right in your face.
Those eyes, the flash of fire like burning pits,
as she ticks off the weary catalogue
of weakness, failings, faults. You *are* a shit.

You see the angle of her hips has grown
sharp beneath her shift, she's little more
than recrimination, skin and bone:
a slip of that girl that once she was,
a flap of flesh where breast had been.
(Through the fear, the shadow of those tits
– magnificent in her time! Low-cut, she cut
through parties like a prow – D-cupped and proud of it).
And this is it – she's a ghost, and you, you're thinking *this*!
She's right. You really are a Grade A Shit.
Question is: How can you lay your lover's ghost?

ii. Big Sleep

... not fall, more like,
two thousand years later at dawn, I stumble into sleep;
splash dry its shallows, puddles, nothing very deep.

And, when I do, I have those dreams.
You know the ones – the past crowds in:
the ones I loved, betrayed, the girl I left for dead,
they're all there, with cocktails, smoking cigarettes;
joking, laughing, partying around my bed.
And I can't move my limbs – I'm wedged in tight
by wood and silk. Something flickers. It's candlelight
and, it slowly dawns on my thick skull,
what it is I'm in
is a coffin.

I am a wake. I am a wake...
... next thing, this morning,
I've got the Buddha speaking in my ear: *I am awake.*
Turns out some academic on *Start The Week.*
And I'm thinking it's time to quit this job, this town
– check that quote this afternoon –
get myself back to where I was,
kneel at that crossroads,
say a prayer, bury this guilty load,
then strike on out, down that other road.

Maybe then,
given a week or two of long days' marches,
I'll sleep more easy.
When it comes to this world of care,
each night be good and dead.
Won't find me there, these hungry ghosts.
Let me die in a stranger's bed.

Three Poems by Sam Gardiner

Second Person

You rush into the shopping arcade
and step aside to avoid the mirror-clad pillar
when you meet yourself rushing out.

Swiftly you pass, and may even glance
over your shoulder just in time to glimpse
yourself spinning on your heel,

wondering which of you is real. As I did,
before hurrying off, getting home first
and trying to persuade her there was only one

of me. But apparently she had always known
there were two, and the one she loved
should soon be home, if I'd care to wait.

A Ring

Ring me, she said, years ago, before this ring,
This remembering. Soon she was coming round
And round, and the polarity was changing
From change in the air to bodies on the ground,
Bodies only, carefree and freestyle night
After night, shocked at not being appalled
At the shock of our animality, the feral cries;
That cry from the bathroom: your Hot is cold!
Cold hands in those days couldn't stop her
Stopping my blues guitar. No No, she'd moan,
And as two noes make one yes I did, never
Expecting ever hand in hand to turn to arm in
Arm, to tongue in cheek. The old fairground
Is fair game for ghosts, white stars hanging
Unchanged, while merrily we two go round
And round, the light catching her ring.

Brick Worker

A brick remembers being earth, being chosen,
and when clean, well-fired and struck
with a trowel or bolster, sings like a pewter mug.

Six thousand years since an Iraqui god
created bricks – and brickies – and still a hodman
hods up and down a ladder, and unbuilds
a pallet by throwing bricks to his mate
on scaffolding two storeys above, who picks them
out of the air, each at the exact apex

of its parabola, and stacks them lightly on the deck.
Anonymous as his life's work, he shies
steel wall-ties into a sack: twenty-three, twenty-four.

The wall the writing was on was brick, he says,
but a good wall tells it all, needs no graffiti,
no BELSHAZZAR YOUR TIME IS UP,
no black airbrush, to spell out the stony sermon.
If there are texts that say more than textures
he'd give his two right arms to see them.

Cloth cap scorched black not by lightning
but by a welder's torch, he stands his ground
behind the headman who ordered his tribe

to stay put and call on the seed to keep its promise.
He climbs into the sky, and slowly raises a wall
behind him, and those who shelter here
will never know this man whose hands know bricks,
who butters, beds and points enough of them
to leave more proof of his being here than most.

Two Poems by Chris Greenhalgh

Last Days

Some messages you don't erase.

My mobile glows like a firefly in the dark.
The moment holds the whole of my life.

My dad, his knackers trapped
in a deckchair
on Blackpool sands, circa 1973.

Or the twang –
that elastic sound the pan made
as it hit against the tap,
its metal note
bending the air,
as he washed my hair...

And for years
I thought death was like that time
in the Blue John mines
they switched off the lights
to leave us in absolute blackness
with only the slow echoey drip from a stalactite
to signal the passing of
millions of years.

He no longer seems located in space –
instead space snags around him.

The last thing he does: record
programmes he knows he'll never see:
Harold Lloyd clinging on
to a giant clock
above the teeming streets.

I see him now, waving from the front step,
his face in the rearview mirror a moon
ghostly in a blue sky –
and his waving doesn't stop
but keeps on
the way he'd say goodbye
over and over on the phone
until finally
I put it down.

On the Shiants

A mid-life crisis drives some to fast cars
and affairs, but it transports me to
a Hebridean isle, along with Robert and Adam, where
there's no running water, toilet, electricity,
no Caffè Nero, fridge or wi-fi – only
whippy grass, guillemots and guano,
and the wind and sea trading blows.

The sea is all volume and no form, though,
as Adam says, an island is enlarged by
the scale of what surrounds it – just as we
are enlarged by his hospitality,
just as sunlight hits the tips of the wind-crimped grass
and glitters, touching the headland like a thought.

A thought? Robert is fifty – which means what?
That he has been around the sun fifty times.
And here we are with our sons, all men together
in the world's second-largest shaggery,
seabirds weeping above the nicked cliffs
and salty dazzle.
        The sky, like a hand,
presses down on a boneyard of buoys, ropes,
driftwood, plastic bottles, razorbills, feathers.
A lit strip of sea gleams between ripped
bits of cloud like a glimpse of the infinite.

We may have lost faith but we retain
the attitude of worshippers
at cathedralic caves, ancient stones,
clear spring water.

At night we retreat
to a warm kitchen, its steam and wine
and talk, where we take the measure
of each other the way children take pleasure
in the clatter of stones.
Here we hatch plans,
plot our stratagems for happiness:
fine wine, a northern fastness,
butter melting with garlic in a pan
and a mobile phone switched off.

Then to our tents, where the wind snags on
an absence, and the sea whitens,
churns – our sleep attuned to its susurration,
our dreams aligned in the small hours with the dip
and sway of the waves, the world
receding like a series of peaks –
bluish, growing paler, forever out of reach.

Three Poems by Ian Gregson

Breaking the Ice

Your fretting about the welfare
of the whole planet jars between us.
I make a charge to brace myself for
spinning high above the ice.
We're skating on a lovely day.
The star that starts to shine is Venus
but you say what shines is sulphur,
Venus shines through acid clouds.
My love of fun you say is just display.
You giggle. Yes. You like my style.
I leap and spin a pirouette
on ice that's shining like a smile
below that scorched erotic star.
The breeze adores us it's so wet
so warm the ice begins to sweat.
I've pushed beyond – it's like a drive
to twist this frenzied spin,
to spin at the top
of my leap, I'm so alive
I'm infectious: you can't stop
yourself from joining in.

The Elastic Band

England became an elastic band,
stretched itself further and further
over raw mountains and whelming sand,
heathen terrain and primitive weather,

frayed its elastic on craggy peaks,
snagged it on jungles, soaked it in seas,
hacked at by Afghans, hacked at by Sikhs –
always and everywhere, new enemies:

These few, these happy few, this band of brothers,
this band could play *God Save the Queen,*
taught the tune to exotic races
but heard in their own thoughts those others
mix a strain of English which would mean
the elastic snapped back in our faces.

The Great Escape

After school he'll visit his grandfather
Who used to be a prisoner of war.
The people move so freely outside the home –
With wincing care, inside, and slow Zimmer frames.

Surely this can't hold his grandfather:
He'll escape his neighbour who complains
Someone's been digging her grave all night,
That her bifocals throw the ground into her eyes.

A prisoner of war like his grandfather
Can dig his way into the youthful streets.
So near he's come but his abandoned tunnels
Veered into sewers and electric cables:

Once you're under, sighs his grandfather, –
Ask the dead – it's hard to climb back up:
Often they find a gutter guarded by bars.
But always he finds his friends down there, his wife,

Mother and father, grandmothers and grandfathers,
And the colours of the waiting Spring.
He's looking forward to the past
His dig unearths like storeys under the floor:

The soil reaches out towards his grandfather,
Heaps of darkness growing under his bed,
The soil in daylight weights his holed pockets
But sprinkles from him, lightening his burden,

Preparing the release of his grandfather –
Downwards and then up. Out of biology
The escaping grandson gallops, frowning
At sunlight, clutching a sparkling Easter egg.

Three Poems by T.F. Griffin

The Canal

If all else was still
We would have come to this place
From a lattice past
And you would be my centre;
Then I too would be your centre:
And we, knowing there was nothing
But an outward circle
And a still home
Would be like two grey swans;
But on the canal, the swans, like us
Move in bruised water.

The Climb

If I came down from Pendle Hill
Into the punishing rain,
And fought my way through Sabden
Into another morning
I would find a hard and clear day;
I would leave the echoes of the mist
And listen to the noises
Of you not returning;
But I have put a distance
Between the day
And the altarless night –
It is both punishment
And the reality of dream;
Listen to what sounds come
From this perpetual stance,
What enigmas.

Winter Sun

Winter sun falls
Through a window
Onto a tired
But happy man.

Outside, the January blossom
From a Japanese Cherry Tree
Makes him think
Of his young lover,
Placing a simple plant
On her mother's grave.

And he knows
That she now knows
Things that he knows.

As his mind opens
Like a flower,
He sees, at last,
The forming
Of a complete circle.

Three Poems by Douglas Houston

Sunday on the Cuillin
For Alan Isherwood

I am becoming wild up here
Among the lichened gabbro,
With my minor infections
And unruly appetites.
I have shed the customary,
Lived on the like of dried fruit and oatcakes,
Gulped the shining water
That spills in sunlight from turquoise pools.

Now I am up on that black ridge
Flanked with ageing snowfields,
Whose prospect had me desolate on arrival.

As the sky's engines haul on worse weather,
I'm about to meet Mr Isherwood,
Who knows the way,
Who forgets it undaunted,
Who is neither too reserved nor too friendly,
And is the gift of my place in a pair.

We proceed in sleet
Down the long rock wedge
Of Sgurr nan Gillean's west ridge
To halt at a gap with lethal drops;
I lead through in about five moves,
Acquiring half way the knowledge
That panic is the option not to be chosen
And am glad to see you not choose it.
Well-matched, indeed, Mr Isherwood,
Our bits of talk, small swops of food,
Three summits plus the sodden miles
Across the moor back to your car,
Where names at last occur to us
And your whisky flask softens weariness
To ease adrift in the blood's warm stream.
Goodbye, Mr Isherwood, driving to mass
Twelve miles away and in a hurry.
The solitude you civilized resumes,
Better for knowing you, poised on the sense
That we'll probably never meet again,
Though tracks and chances might allow we will,
Some other day, some other hill.

Shackleton et Fils

Out on the empty beach he plays with verse
Much as his infant son does with the sand,
Observes that here his mood seems to expand
Till rhythm's buoyancy dispels the curse
And parodies of Wordsworth intersperse
The silences between events that stand
Autonomous as purposes disband;
The day's a blank where language may rehearse
Its tendencies to organize round sound,
Extravagant and aureate, facile, flowing,
Uttered and lost with no one to confound
This talent the unconscious is bestowing
In sweet encounters with the air around
A beach they like and leave with nothing owing.

Your Only Man

Your only man subdues the dialogue,
Gets it so quiet that you barely notice,
And find the fluting on plastic lampposts
More interesting in the free afternoon
Than conscience and justice babbling
Their representations in the chamber
That seems to be located in your head.

On the bus, you are borne through a while in late June –
All that green bringing forth flower and seed –
Agreeably warm under seamless cloud.
Ought and do are lulled half-asleep
By the gently modulated hum
From tyres on tarmac and continuous traction
Pulling through the geared registers.

Your only man makes sure the ride is good,
Keeps all concerned away from the genitive,
Distracts with well-timed prompts to look at
Weathered stonework and rife vegetation.
The game, he reminds you, has simple rules,
Then opens his hand when you mention the future,
As if to say 'You may not need me then'.

Three Poems by Margot K. Juby

Les Très Riches Heures de Gilles de Rais

The leather binding is curious,
soft and pale, of no known provenance.

Its silver clasps have tarnished into blackness,
grim as coffin furbishments.

The key is rusted red, like Bluebeard's key
indelibly stained with blood.

Inside, the pigments glow from the page
in formal miniatures, vermilion, gold.

Argent on a ground of sable
a unicorn rampant rears its horn.

Here is a serpent the size of a dog
and there a leopard with human eyes.

A heap of gold transmuting into leaves,
the heart of a child in a jewelled monstrance.

A black stake and a pile of kindling,
the white face of a virgin martyr burning.

A crowd looks on, as blank as playing cards.
The licking flames seem cool, like amber.

A human figure is split down its axis;
half gilded girl, half crowned and bearded male.

A hawk-faced Herod in his purple watches
the scarlet tableau of innocents slaughtered.

There are geometrical fountains of blood.
From the sky, blond angels look down, impassive.

A grey river crawls through a watery landscape;
three gibbets, tenanted, stand framed by fire.

A phoenix in his crimson glory poises
resurgent above a pyre of blackened bone.

Crow Town

This is a crow town –
there are no magpies round here.
Solid black from beak to tailfeather.

We don't do your fancy
piebald glad rags.
We don't talk your poncy language.

We do your straight
evisceration of live fledglings
while the mother squawks.

No frills, no grace-notes.
We don't go for bright gewgaws
or pinch girls' earrings.

We don't mince about in tidings;
when we gang up
they call it murder.

We don't bring bad luck
or good either.
Nobody bows and sucks up to us.

Nobody jabbers silly rhymes.
This is a crow town
where crows live and do crow things.

We want no magpies round here.

The Blood-Red Tattoo

My grandfather had tattoos –
they crept up his arms like a blueish mould.
I didn't want mine done like that,
so faded and antique.

Nor did I want stark Celtic black –
too harsh for my white skin.
I had your signature done in crimson
just where the elbow bends.

As if I'd cut it in my softest flesh
and drawn my heart's vermilion blood.
As if you'd signed your name
with loving brutality and a straight razor.

This is my one tattoo:
I need no other. It stamps me yours –
branded, wounded, bought and paid for,
signed and sealed by your own hand.

It itches, sometimes; as if you stroked it.

Two Poems by David Kennedy

From: <philip1897@yahoo.com>
Subject:Arc

· Dear friend ·
· I am a human being like you ·
· century/sensory overload ·
· but it seems that things is not flowing well ·
· the way it suppose ·
· vast siestas of climate change ·
· 459 parts per million ·
· that is why you see some advance men ·
· going the way they do not suppose in order to balance ·
· so universall a distemperature ·
· that is why you see 5 pods painted Reckitt's blue ·
· 23 powerbooks uplifted ·
· pray for us hear us deliver us ·
· sixteen turbines whirring ·
· tuning the wind to our times ·
· that is why ·
· back and forth between nature and culture ·
· air flows across a trough of cool water ·
· back and forth between outer and inner ·
· that is why you see ·
· a shelter and forest ·
· in circuits of the common air light and water ·
· recalling the earth intemerata ·

· some advance men going the way ·
· they do not suppose have made ·
· a forcework ·
· being unfolding ·
· forces freed into becoming ·
· a place of transformation ·
· people enter the building ·
· a moveable prayer ·
· people are reorganized through natural forces ·
· people are changed and charged ·
· so they go out the way they do not suppose ·
· to other the balance of their living ·
· that is why you see what you see ·
· a wedge ·
· keeping the door of the future ajar ·
· this motion came to me after I went to arc ·
· a building that is modest and extrovert ·
· after I went through arc ·
· where relations unfold outside ·
· the usual forms and operations of power ·
· what I need is help from you ·
· only you can make a little step to achieve it ·
· thanks and regards ·

The Hull Emigration Platform

A waiting room and a platform,
separate spaces so alien saying
didn't interrupt the city's solid said.

The platform is desire. The platform is loss.

A waiting room and a platform.
There is a kind of weather here,
the weather of saying.

Perronen er længsel. Perronen er savn.

The platform points its consecutive form
into the future where the air sifts and the air
sifts and the light lifts and lifts.

Asemalaituri on kaipus. Asemalaituri on menetys.

There were songs that became old keys,
sources of rivers, cables laid under oceans,
tastes of fruit, scents of soil,
grandfather in a straw hat standing with a horse.

Der Bahnsteig ist Sehnsucht. Der Bahnsteig ist Verlust.

There were whole worlds not 50 miles from home;
then cart to train to ship to train to train to ship
and the challenge to go on liking what you are
in the face of doubts cast on your own definition.

Perrongen er lengsel. Perrongen er savn.

There are words that move with their speakers:
here, there, past, future, light, summer, water.

Platforma – eto zhelanie. Platforma – eto poteria.

And then there were children and grandchildren
who knew the look and position
of every property in villages they had never visited.

Perrongen är längtan. Perrongen är saknad.

There is a kind of weather here.
It all comes together looking.
There is a platform. The direction in which it points.
Open room for the saying.

Three Poems by Angela Leighton

Windfall

An ill wind, misprint or flaw,
a fault in the workings, trouble on a face,

like the boy's autistic stare as he stood,
that hurt wonder breaking his logic –

Back, he begged. *Put it back*, and showed
how easily the break might join –

a snapped toy, the greenery foiled,
an apple fallen in the way of things.

And I, turning, saw a garden of windfalls –
root and branch, graft and stock,

from too far back to know the cause –
smashed on the grass, sweetening the soil.

So that, at a loss for all the world,
for damage done at the heart of it,

the knot, the quirk, reverse and fall,
I reached for what I could not mend:

that small hand, not mine, in my own,
and sang, for the rhyme's sake, 'We all fall down.'

Form
(after Hepworth's *Orpheus*)

Let there be – a form in the seeing,
block-carved, tilt-centred, handy maquette,
its cusp ghosting light's emptiness.

Let there be – grosgrain or roughening,
the patina left on inflected brass,
from horn or harp, a graph of strings.

Let there be – the hint of a caress
open to pure air, a gesture expressed,
flex to Hades–touch and forget.

Let there be – formality, finish,
a space that's strung, a stillness tensing,
cut to the quick, but still turned, listening.

Sortilege

They grow to forgetful hands, fasten in fists,
quick-foot it into our shoes, hitching a lift,
then see through themselves in a mirror, furtive chancers,
cleared, lost to the world, tricks of the weather.

Their make-up makes us up, their genes inflect,
and givens seem a gift, a kind of luck.
They gravitate through us, from smile to cry
still staring out in wonder from our eyes.

A fright, I tell myself, and touch to know
the mirror's cold assertion, half my own.
The dead come home to us, their last resort.
My face is yours, re-formed, a home of sorts.

Two Poems by Frances Leviston

Story

Under what tree, in what part of the forest, beside which branch
of the leaf-obstructed stream, in sun or in rain,

concreted into what foundation, supporting whose house, deaf
to how many dinner parties, subjected to how many holding-forths,

compacted along with what model of car, with what registration,
wearing which perfume and what sort of pearls,

in the back-of-beyond of what country, adjoining whose under-
development land, masked by which strain of animal fodder's

pollen blown from the next field along, belonging to whom, missed
by whom, questioned by which particular method, scarred where,

repaired where, reopened how, broken how,
how *taken care of*, transported how, buried

how, in what manner and from what platform disclaimed
during which international crisis, during which electoral year,

under whose watch, under whose watch
and why will it surface, why will it then be permitted to surface,

the end of the story, the body we need?

Sight

That winter drift-trapped in the house,
learning the campfire of flesh and the endless
tether the mind ranges upon,

I came into the living room and saw
a glass jug suspended in the air, six feet clear
of the carpet, tipped. There were no wires,

no mirror tricks. The whole world hung
on whatever invisible hook or hand
was keeping it tilted, empty, gleaming.

I stepped towards it, as if in a dream. It fell
as the rain falls, suddenly out of
the sky's indifference, and shattered at once.

Two Poems by Roger McGough

An Apology

Sincere apologies, too late I know, for not getting engaged
on the night we'd planned, Christmas Eve 1962. I had
   the ring
in my pocket, the one we'd chosen together in November
from the little jewellers on Whitefriargate. Remember?

After Midnight Mass arm-in-arming back to ours,
we linger outside the gates of Seaforth Park. The moon
smiling and expectant. No wind, no people, no cars.
Sheets of ice are nailed to the streets with stars.

The scene is set, two lovers on the silver screen.
A pause, the copy-book kiss. Did angels sing?
This was my moment, the cue to pledge my troth.
To take out the blue, velvet box, and do my stuff.

But marriage was a bridge I feared might be detonated,
and I had this crazy idea that if I didn't mention it,
then you wouldn't either. That we'd collude in romantic
   amnesia.
That life would go on as before. What could be easier?

Christmas passed. Enraged, you blew up.
I felt the blast.
We got engaged. It didn't last.

'What Does Your Father Do?'

At university, how that artful question embarrassed me.
In the common-room, coffee cup balancing on cavalry twills,
some bright spark (usually Sociology) would want an answer.
Shame on me, as feigning lofty disinterest, I would hesitate.

Should I mumble 'docker' in the hope of being misheard?
('There he goes, a doctor's son, and every inch the medical man')
Or should I pick up the hook and throw it down like a gauntlet?
'Docker. My dad's a docker.' A whistle of corduroy.

How about? 'He's a stevedore, from the Spanish *estibador*
meaning packer, or loader, as in ship'. No, sounds too
On the Waterfront, and dad was no Marlon Brando.
Besides, it's the handle they want, not the etymology.

'He's a foreman on the docks.' A hint of status? Possibly.
A touch of class? Hardly. Better go with the straightforward
'He works on the docks in Liverpool,' which leaves it open.
Crane-driver? Customs and Excise Officer? Canteen Manager?

Clerk? Chairman of the Mersey Docks and Harbour Board?
In dreams now, I hear him naming the docks he knew and loved.
A mantra of gentle reproach. *Gladstone, Hornby, Alexandra,*
Langton, Brocklebank, Canada, Huskisson, Sandon, Wellington,

Bramley Moor, Nelson, Salisbury, Trafalgar, Victoria.......

Three Poems by Andrew Motion

The Korean Memorial at Hiroshima

There was hardly time
between the Peace Museum
and the bullet train to Tokyo,
but our hosts instructed the taxi
to find the memorial to the Koreans.
Ten thousand Koreans, killed that morning.
You, being Korean, had to see it.

*

We had been crying in the Museum:
the charred school uniforms;
the lunch-box with its meal of charcoal,
the shadow of a seated woman
printed on the steps of a bank.
Everyone else was crying, too.
We shuffled round in a queue,
crying and saying nothing.

Then we stood in the rain
squaring up to the Memorial.
A spike of rusty flowers
and a tide-scum of dead cherry blossom.
Five or six miniature ceremonial costumes
made of folded paper and left to moulder.
Pink. Pink and custard yellow.
You could hardly leave soon enough.

*

The taxi was on its last legs,
sputtering among black cherries
then stalling by the skeleton
of the one dome to survive the blast.

No need to worry about the train, though.
The trains in Japan run on time.
In two hours and fifteen minutes
we would see Mount Fuji,
cloud-cover permitting,
and the snow-cap like a table-cloth
stretched over a tumbler of water
in the moment of surprise
before a magician taps his wand
and the tumbler disappears.

Over Here

Eventually I decided on the field
planted with winter wheat, although
the farmer would crucify me if he saw.

It was all down to my kite needing
space not possible in our valley,
except the ground was sodden,

and a trek to the centre hard going.
A peewit kept me company, broken-
winged and weeping *Over here!*

tempting me into some act of violence.
Never mind, as long as her plan saved
the nest with its clutch of delicious eggs.

The New York Planetarium

At the beginning of our life together
we went to the New York Planetarium.

It was our childhood, or something close.
The sky-dome was too vast for comfort

and so, to reveal its great beauty entirely,
they gave us seats which tilted backwards.

Then we and everyone else stopped talking
and listened to Charlton Heston, whose voice

rose like God's to fill the star-spangled dark.
It was impressive, but the sight of your hair

pouring straight and sleek and completely black
across the arched red velvet of your chair-back

was even more startling. Then I looked up again.
The two massive galaxies now visible overhead

continued to draw more closely to one another
with a very clear promise from Charlton Heston

that eventually they would collide. It meant
almost nothing to me. When your face turned

in wonder from one part of the known universe
to the next, lights no less bright than the stars

scattered over your hair like cold fire arriving
from thousands and thousands of miles away.

Three Poems by Grace Nichols

Outward from Hull

The gulls of Hull
the train pulling out –
a metallic snake
along the estuary
leaving behind
the forceful ghost
of Wilberforce
the confluence
of the Hull and the Humber.
Brough, Selby, Doncaster.
How many times
have I sat this way
England, gazing out
at the leafless names
of trees; at cathedrals
I still haven't seen –
our inter-city boa
pushing through
the deepening night –
the wet black roots
of the country.
Suddenly, for some
unearthly reason,
it falters, then stops –
an inexplicable
paralysis of rhythm –
the brooch of a small
town gleaming
in the distance –
the eels and eels
of branching tracks.

O England –
hedge-bound as Larkin
omnivorous as Shakespeare.

Advice on Crossing a Street in Delhi

First take a few moments to observe
the traffic's wayward symmetry.

While contemplating wheels of mortality,
note how whole families on motorbikes
dart daring within the shifting shoal
of the cacophonous river.

Surely if they can, you too can
weave a quick trajectory
So go –
at the first signs of a small break
with a great faith and a great surrender.

If stranded in the middle of the road
become a sacred cow with gilded horns
adopting the inner stillness of the lotus posture.
Let honking cars, rickshaws, lorries,
swarm or fly around you.

You are in the hands of the great mother.
The thing about India maybe
is to get the rhythm right –
this rhythm that will change the way
you cross a street forever.

A Statement From
The Empire State Building

Still stately standing (thank God) ton on ton
Still intact with the image of my clinging Kong.
Part of this Lego-dream of gold and dark –
Times Square; Madison Square Garden;
Brooklyn Bridge; the haunting voice
of that busker's song drifting out
below the girders into the Hudson;
and all eyes returning to me like moths
now that the twin-kingdoms have gone.
I hold each flame-lit window they beat
against – a miniature Fort Knox.
But tonight, tonight, the crescent new moon
so close beside my antenna's pulsing star
stirs me down to my steel bones,
its ancient cryptic formation
awakening in me a thirst for desert.
Now I'm as light as a buoy
dragging my bedrock-roots across the ocean –
reaching out an art-deco hand
towards the minarets of those mosques;
enquiring if they too quaked when terror
rained its righteousness from our planes?
O to be a ship
on this night of crescent moon and pulsing star
sailing far – from earth's tragic empires.

Three Poems by Sean O'Brien

The Citizens

We change the river's name to make it ours.
We wall the city off and call it fate.
We husband our estate of ash,
For what we have we hold, and this
Is what is meant by history.
We have no love for one another, only uses
We can make of the defeated.
– And meanwhile you have disappeared
Like smoke across a frozen field.

What language? You had no language.
Stirring bone soup with a bone, we sip
From the cup of the skull. This is culture.
All we want to do is live forever,
To which end we make you bow down to our gods
In the midday square's Apollonian light
Before we ship you to the furnaces
And sow you in the fields like salt
So that nothing will grow there but death.

We fear that the fields of blue air at the world's end
Will be the only court we face.
We fear that when we reach the gate alone
There will be neither words nor deeds
To answer with. Therefore, we say, let us
Speak not of murder but of sacrifice,
And out of sacrifice make duty,
And out of duty love,
Whose name, in our language, means death.

Blizzard

The snow will bring the world indoors, the fall
That saves the Gulf Stream and the Greenland Shelf.
White abolitionist of maps and calendars,
Its Lenten rigour pillowed like a sin, it means
To be the only season, falling always on itself.
To put an end to all analogy, pure cold
That proves what it need never say,
It calls us home again beneath a drift
In which the figure and the ground collapse –
No more of metaphor, no more perhaps.

Look at these attic windowsills, look in the grate –
White after white against the off-white sheets,
The wafers of a pitiless communion
That turns a wood to Mother Russia and the night
To afterlife, then to a snowblind street.
With cataracts and snow-tipped breasts
The mermaids in their brazen lingerie
Wait bravely at the fountain in the square.
Green girls, they think it is their destiny
To offer the ideal to empty air.

Forgive me that I did not understand
That you were actual, not merely art,
That your fidelity was courage, that I failed
To honour you, to recognize your pain,
To grasp that snow once fallen will not fall again.
Now it grows clear: the world is not a place
But an occasion, first of sin and then the wish
That such self-knowledge may be recognized,
While snow continues falling, while we learn
That there is neither punishment nor grace.

Fantasia on a Theme of James Wright

There are miners still
In the underground rivers
Of West Moor and Palmersville.

There are guttering cap-lamps bound up in the roots
Where the coal is beginning again.
They are sinking slowly further

In between the shiftless seams,
To black pools in the bed of the world.
In their long home the miners are labouring still –

Gargling dust, going down in good order,
Their black-braided banners aloft,
Into flooding and firedamp, there to inherit

Once more the tiny corridors of the immense estate
They line with prints of Hedley's *Coming Home*.
We hardly hear of them.

There are the faint reports of spent economies,
Explosions in the ocean floor,
The thud of iron doors sealed once for all

On prayers and lamentation,
On pragmatism and the long noyade
Of a class which dreamed itself

Immortalized by want if nothing else.
The singing of the dead inside the earth
Is like the friction of great stones, or like the rush

Of water into newly opened darkness. Oh my brothers,
The living will never persuade them
That matters are otherwise, history done.

One Poem and a Sequence
by Caitríona O'Reilly

Now or When
On the sundial at Beverley Minster

All of my days fall into this easy measure.
The sun in his ecliptic marks me, as candles
describing lucent circles in the dark. From my
high place on the wall I have seen the down-at-heels
pass in their own cycles, imagining their flesh
cold and perishable as the moon, my other
light. Moss overgrows me, and from my crumbling mouth
mottoes drop implacable as stones. *Nobody
looks at me when the sun is not there.* Is it good
always to say the same thing? My tilt no longer
mirrors the world's, or the calculations have changed.
The last is hidden so we have to watch them all.
Every decade since, his path has been removing,
his meridian eluding me, rooted here
unmoving and unmoved. *O light, I hope for thee
in this darkness.* I pray this earthly pendulum
swings back towards its first innocent embroidery
of stars – *time is an arrow that flieth* – and I
can regain my zenith. *Remember life is short.*

A Quartet for the Falcon

I *The Mews*

My falcon is snatched from the air.
It is the dark time. I have cast
sweet-smelling rushes on the floor
and the walls are unlimed.

I keep a lamp burning in here.
Outside, England dreams under
a mantle of legendary snow,
her trees stood bare, aghast,

her spine stiffened against winter.
History is yet to happen.
I have banished the tercel-gentle
beyond hearing, while my lady

waits her change.
I have hidden her creance and bells
sounding their chord of freedom;
her buttercup feet keep the perch.

Twenty nights I waked her, haggard,
till she flew to the lure and stooped in air
to dive into my flittered dreams,
fixing them with her stares and ways.

Now I have seeled her eyes again,
hiding their black beams
with a stitch to each golden underlid,
knotting the threads behind.

She cannot see the spider twitch
on the rafter, nor the lamp's slow flicker.
She is blind to her own change
as all men are but I, witnessing

the colours drop from her breast,
the mineral glint of her back
go shabby as the waned moon
under a tonneweight of shed feathers.

II *Opus Contra Naturam*

I feed her decoction of diamond-skinned adder,
hawker's prophylaxis, proof against taint in the wing.
That she should absorb the snake's cunning
makes me her alchemist, rattling the atoms
on a vitreous well. Red sulphur, argent vive, even
I, I, I, trichloro-2, 2bis (parachlorophenyl) ethane:
solve et coagula. Behold the work of my hands –
dead metals litter the ground, my poor bird sickens
and will not rise until warmed by a flame to the limbeck.
I have made a sealed world to hatch heavenly birds,
their flight a cloud-burst, a rain of mercurial feathers,
while outside the peregrine atom wanders
through field, seed and leaf, and through the egg's
chamber: thin-shelled and toxic on the eyrie's edge.

III *The Lure*

Snared in a mode of seeing,
the raptor's eyes unseel again.

Not an outline scarfing the blue wind
but several worlds unscrolling:

the chemical plant's logical conduits
glitter like the keys of a flute

while brown earth casts up
bones of its lost alluvial people:

shards of Delft in a Dutch landscape.
Abandoned churches ride the horizon

like high ships. She is caught in the rigging –
such details as flowers in dark grass,

calligraphic wings imped by a scribe
to *fiat lux,* or mantling their Marian prey.

Over a bleached Segovian plain the eye
seeks its eagle like the sky's pupil.

Aguila, describing a brutal circle.
Slow clouds tumble from the cooling stacks.

Anchor, tear-drop and cut diamond –
now her sentimental silhouette descends

to a swung horseshoe bound in leather.
It is the World, the Flesh, the Devil.

IV *The Curée*

The secretive hart turns at bay,
lowers his tines to the hounds' cry.
The sword enters the bull's heart –
　　　still he stands,
　　　amazed on the red sand
as the stony unbeliever might,

who has seen God. Soon now
horns will sound *dedow*
for the unmaking. Beaters flush
　　　the grey heron
　　　like a coney from its warren,
the peregrine's jet eyes flash.

They go ringing up the air,
each in its separate spiral stair
to the indigo rim of the skies,
　　　then descend
　　　swift as a murderer's hand
with a knife. Death's gesture liquefies

in bringing the priestly heron down.
Her prize, the marrow from a wing-bone
in which she delights, her spurred
　　　fleur-de-lys tongue
　　　stained *gold-vermilion* –
little angel in her hangman's hood.

Three Poems by Ian Parks

North Landing

Strange that I should find myself with you
on this abandoned headland skimming stones.
The ones you choose skip once or twice then sink;
mine skitter on the surface, disappear.
Stranger still to chance on something new
at fifty when the tide begins to turn.

They say each smooth white pebble holds a soul
that shatters when you split its heart in two.
The beach is full of broken hearts –
each inlet and each cove alive and echoing,
their secret chambers domed and stratified.
This late in the season, this late in the day

I start to think such stories might be true.
And when souls lost at sea need rescuing
they launch the lifeboat and its grim-faced crew
on a frantic, runaway white-knuckle ride
down the steep chute with the rusted rails,
into the cold and unresisting spray.

Lazarus

After I brought you back to life
your short death made you frightened of the sun.
I knelt above you, rolled away the stone,

uncoiled the silken thread that filled your throat.
You never caught my whisper, never saw me when I wept.
I called you from the darkness and you came.

You came expecting birdsong, a new world.
Instead, I hauled you up and set you down,
dragged you back choking from the brink.

The others kept their distance, hid their eyes,
refused to hear the flutter of your heart.
You stuttered, disappointed that the world was still the
    same.

I acted quickly, breathed into your mouth –
astonished as your blue lips turned to red.
I learned your secret, kept it to myself,

stood silent as you stumbled from the cave.
I loved you for returning, for the effort that you'd made.
You hated me for doing what I'd done.

Downpour

Not the rain that Edward Thomas heard
beating on the roof of his tin hut
but heavy-sheeted, unrelenting rain
that drives across the landscape that he loved.

To have that sort of rain, you'd need
to change the places that it falls upon –
unbuild the office blocks and shopping malls,
tear down the children's playgrounds, roundabouts

and disinvent the electronic chip.
You'd need to clear the motorways,
break up the concrete car parks,
make them ready for the plough.

Let the rain rain unimpeded on
the nettles and the curled up ferns.
For that you'd need to change the hearts
and ears of those it rained upon;

make sensitive the taproot and the soil.
Not the rain that Edward Thomas heard –
the rain that rinses as it falls.
This rain has acid in it and it burns.

Three Poems by Tom Paulin

A Single Weather
(Khazendar)

They've got gaps in them the best walls
– it was a geg the way we'd grip hands
then slip through that tall – tall
and tight – gap in the wall
yes we squinched through that fissure
came back again and again we did
under fruit that was fit to burst

I could hear you trapped in your own voice
as we made sleaked talk – worse and worse –
by a well that since we were kids
no one'd drawn a bucket from ever
– unlike the sky you were never the same
and come nightfall you were different again
you felt no right to go back – both it
and the will to return
you'd let slip

Matins

A tinniness in that bell
– I was ten when I heard it first
its sad but urgent tang
binging across two dead –
you could hardly call them fields
and there it goes again
off-key but beating out
its meek unsettled belief
on a shore of this small republic
not a *cloche fêlée* for sure
just Anglican Irish and poor

maybe I'll cross those acres
– deadness and brambles just
between our home and the church?
go into that half-strange porch
its odour of damp and limewash
strawbottomed chairs and slack
well loose little case of hymnals
it must be a tribal thing
this wanting to go back there
(d'you want to kneel in prayer?)
this wishing the words were firm
with a bit of a kick and a skip
why couldn't they stay the same
and sing *bing-ding bing-ding*?

Settlers

They cross from Glasgow to a black city
  Of gantries, mills and steeples. They begin to belong.
He manages the Iceworks, is an elder of the Kirk;
  She becomes, briefly, a nurse in Carson's Army.
Some mornings, walking through the company gate,
  He touches the bonnet of a brown lorry.
It is warm. The men watch and say nothing.
  'Queer, how it runs off in the night,'
He says to McCullough, then climbs to his office.
  He stores a warm knowledge on his palm.

Nightlandings on the Antrim coast, the movement of guns
Now snug in their oiled paper below the floors
  Of sundry kirks and tabernacles in that county.

Two Poems by Tony Petch

Two Poems

Sonnet 1
a sonnet is a poem of fourteen lines
the first eight of which
create tension
the remaining six
being the resolution
the ratio six to eight
approximating the proportions
of an aesthetically ideal rectangle
based on the golden mean
which is actually
more accurately represented
by the fibonacci series
whereby each successive digit
is the sum of the previous two

Sonnet 2
accordingly therefore
a sonnet should more precisely comprise
eight lines
followed by five
making a total instead of only thirteen
and as for feet rhyme and metre
these days this seems pretty arbitrary
in the same way
that the division between tension and resolution
is now often ignored
which brings me to my final point
that the sonnet above has fourteen lines
whilst this sonnet has one line less

The Holding

Instead of a hole the string, or maybe the shed kept
together, an entire garden tied. Hold me you say. I
breathe you in, a bud opening. So close to a rose could be
nothing. And how far are we? The original kept warm yet
thin, the waist wasted if it's not as elegant as the string.
Yellow and black. Yellow and black and the wings, a point
being a corner of the shape where dad leans his spades. A
clarity is both protected and retained. As description, a
plot divided between development and execution. A thorn
in back-to-front. Not buckthorn but hawthorn. To replace
a crop a line of parsnips, the second row to steal from your
worship. Social enquiry means to set a record straight, to
pay the penalty of each paragraph, poor sod. A long way
from stripes round, the sun tanning our backs as we hoe
between the carrots.

Three Poems by Genny Rahtz

Sky Windows

I hear all those flat
open plain vowels
in North American voices,
folk songs, speeches,
gospel, blues, work songs.

I hear their influence
on those who still jump logs
jammed in slow rivers,
keep attention
on the unencumbered present.

I hear the long grain
in Robert Frost and Sharon Olds,
the laconic
slow transatlantic roll
of Black Mountain poets.

I hear the silence
of big distances
in how Mark Rothko colours
change their pitch
and float on ragged boundaries.

I feel the temperature of shadows
in Coen Brothers' films,
eloquent as James Turrell's
sky windows
after images of so much light.

Bird Prints

For years we lived
on the hard surface of a city
beached on the Humber
and of necessity,
absorbed the slow mix
of fresh and salt tides
that draw the margins.

We knew the weight
of territorial bird prints
on silver mud flats.

They have become
hieroglyphs of memory
for all those years
we searched for refuge,
saturated by the light
that bleaches all sense
of distance across the estuary.

Embodied Memory

Every time
I step
from the medium of this dry breath
from land to water
I am reclothed
in the movement of liquid on my skin.
My spine elongates,
extends the breath
to outstretched limbs,
fingers, toes,
awakens embodied memory.

And as I swim,
my breathing, amplified
excites ancient molecules of breath
exhaled
from remote human ancestors...

who fished the tides
and swam with long hair
rising and falling on the sea,
hair dripping
as they searched for driftwood,
climbed barefoot to their caves,
could still hear the crunch
of predator on shingle.

They watched light
changing over the sea,
synchronised their breathing
with the waves,
or sat by firelight
cocooned in slow pulse
tidal rhythms,
boom of sea caves.

Two Poems by Frank Redpath

Story Time

I think that what she said
Involved being nineteen, away from home
To take some kind of test, an interview.
She met an older man, someone who knew
What it was all about, who gave her some
Lunch and some good advice but didn't try it on.

Later, I think, there was
A mix-up with the trains that made her late.
She thought that Deptford (Dartford, was it?) lay
Just down the line from where she had to stay
So trotted off there. Did I get this right?
Something quite frightening, then? A dog that
    snatched her glove?

Disasters, more or less.
At least, I think they were. Remembering such
Details as these is not what I do best.
Partly that while she spoke, I held her breast
Cupped in my hand, partly the rich
Dazzle of what I thought I saw got in the way.

While she was talking I
Kept looking backwards at her in the train:
London approaching like brass instruments
Announcing the arrival of presents
While she prepared for freedom, on her own
In clothes she thought were splendid, and clean underwear.

We meet less often now.
Painful to limp up stairs we used to leap
Three at a time, but sometimes when we do
She holds a dress up. "Look at this, it's new.
Isn't it splendid?" When she does, I hope
That she will always be moving towards that good

She posed for years ago.
Therefore I send her this apology
For poor attention to her complex tales
And to explain that when she does her nails,
Looks round and catches me, and says, "Are you
Laughing at me?" and I say, "Yes" I mean, "Thank you."

How it Turned Out

One I imagined standing on a dark hill, with the lights
  of the city before him,
A sign grown into his hand, a directing pressure
  between his eyes;
Not to be fooled with mirrors, thorn-cruel maybe but vital;
Soon to be shown a dark world, yes, but brimming,
  a busy harbour
With houses lighted and open and dancing about the trees,
And a salesman's twist of the road through, roaring
  from friend to friend round lovely corners.

Was given instead a distorting-glass, a guide in
  broken English
And a sextant but no sun; only, repeatedly, morning
Greyly disgracing him. And, further, was denied
The ability to dance, the hieratic steps
Or the shrugging coward's posture, but was left
Alone on a long road, with a diminishing memory
  of North.

Three Poems by Christopher Reid

Kandy

I can't say that I saw the Tooth itself,
but I did see the bedizened elephant that carried it –
as important a performer, surely, as Chesterton's
    donkey –
and hear the clamour and trumpeting
of the accompanying throng.

Our balcony was high above the road
along which the procession passed like a turbulent river
bearing away an unseen holy relic,
bearing elephants, bearing everything away.

Ink

By mischance, I fell among the drinkers of ink.
I knew them at once by their stained lips, their sour stink
and the light-threatened look in their eyes, a perpetual
half-awake blink.

In their awkward way, they were friendly at first,
offering me a bottle of ink to assuage my traveller's thirst.
I downed it in one gulp and nodded thanks, with my lips
pursed.

You could get used to the taste, I thought, in time, by an
effort of will,
but could you ever, with their apparent relish, swill
gallons of the stuff and not spend all day feeling vibrantly
ill?

To them, however, ink was not just what water is to you
and me;
it was a rich, nutritious broth, a soothing tea,
a courage-boosting liquor and a loving-cup of sacramental
efficacy.

If paper was their staple diet, ink lent
distinction and purpose to their culture. A blue or black
tongue meant
their every utterance had God's unequivocal assent.

I knew my squeamishness would be construed as pride
and hoped it would pass unnoticed, but it was too great
to hide
and before long I was summoned to the temple to have my
appetite tried.

Picture the wrath on the face of the high priest, with his
  indelible
beard of inky dribble,
as he watched me dip the corner of an A4 sheet and take
  a fastidious nibble.

Rising from his throne, jabbing at me with his gold-nibbed
  pen,
he pronounced instant banishment. Roused, his men
shoved and buffeted me as far as the gates, and I was out
  on the road again.

Chorale

The Kapellmeister of Kilnsea
confronts his mutinous choir.

He has a new cantata that he wants them to sing,
but they have a composition of their own

that they're in the middle of now,
and they're not about to interrupt it:

a chorale of absolute din, a multitude-part
white-noise polyphony, almost unhearable

upwhelming basso-profundities
supporting a shoving and tumbling

scrum of unresolved counterpoint
with, at the top, a foamy descant, all ecstatic shatters.

They won't stop. But the Kapellmesiter
is patient. His cantata can wait.

It may even be improved, if he listens with care
and can catch and steal whatever it is

that gives the racket its seeming power and purpose,
and can slip it into the neat score on his desk at home.

Two Poems by Carol Rumens

Elegiac Fragments

I

Nothing is as alive as a private letter
                    however dated
nothing so dead as a grave-stone
                    however recent

  and the poem that rainbows between them?

II

The serious river, the terrible hotel
pretended momentarily
to remember your name.
But in fact they had passed untransformed
among the countless minds that encountered them,
yours included, traceless
millions included. They are so crammed with names
they can't speak: they have nothing to do with speech.

III

The polar-bear, meat-hooked
to the ship's side in the museum photograph,
utters the full weight of defeated dignity.

The dead become things, first heavy, then light   on the way
they catch us through our curtains.
Yeats, Auden wrote, became his admirers.

You became a new brand

IV

Or was it only the bridge of the nose, the eye-sockets?
Well   we will continue dulling the iris
of the language a little longer   until
the commas have dripped away like money
and the garlanded line is as lost as Queen Anne
              lost as the craft
of lace   and unknown the nomenclature of wild flowers
    though a last whisper names
    these cheap ones ours
wasteful   weak yes
              propitiatory? No.

V

Weaving my lines on-screen   I keep seeing
                            the glass-painter
named in the Hammersmith census of 1900:
glitterings in the bay-window   fancy lamp-bits
                                    blobbed
        oils on enamel dishes
bespectacled he frowns   to keep seeing
                    his minuscule brushwork.

VI

the poem is a museum a garland of footnotes to
                                    footnotes
              however recent
the poem is a harpoon   you can't remove it
                  however dated.

(Note: Italicised words are from 'The Building,' Philip Larkin,
The Whitsun Weddings, 1972.)

The Cinque Terre

*('Years of cliffs and horizons shaped /
to shelter lives still human...')*

To shelter lives still humam
the rock rears up, kicks out, gyrates,
splits its cracked hide with amphi-theatrical
hula-hoops of walls
all going at different speeds, toppling at different angles.

They scramble up the webbed toes, the fissured pendulous
belly –
water-butts, pines, boatmen, shepherds – hooked
to the verges of extinction, roots tucked
into the rock's long outrage. They adjust
their vertigo by stages, and resist.

A poet, like anyone else, learns to cling on
among the ticks and fleas, the dried-up scribbles of
moisture,
all that death-quadrille, for ever changing hands
and broken up by the squirming plates and jagged
sun of Atlantis. Rain is his art, his vocation

to be the storm that sets things flowing, to pour
as the rusting waste-pipes finally
  open their mouths and
     open their
 rusting barbarous mouths and roar
       and lather
     the rain-fugue over
the staves   dislodge or vivify
some shuddering root   and pour

his corrosive, solving *stretto* back to the pounding salt-wash

Note 'Anni di scogli e di orizzonti stretti a custodire vite anocra
umane...' Eugenio Montale, 'Prodi di Versilia', *La Bufera e Altro*,
Tr. Jonathan Galassi. Montale's family originated in Monterosso,
one of the five villages of the Cinque Terre.

Four Poems by Maurice Rutherford

The Cod Farm

I have your photo on my wall
in grainy not-quite-black-and-white,
blown-up, to try to bring you close

The way few sons and fathers are.
The original's in Hull museum –
The Cod Farm: you, flat cap and all,

with cod spread out on racks to dry
salt-white, 'earning a crust' by which
Mum bought that first school uniform

I rolled around the playground in
to make less obviously new
to boys with bigger fists than mine.

'See Maurice, see our Dad again!'
Quite what the others find of you
in me, they don't explain. Bald head;

the less than generous mouth, your voice?
And I don't tell them how I feel
a certain late affinity;

how, since you died, sometimes it seems
it's not my face but yours I shave
(though wrong way round); your faults I see

mirrored in me – like how I use
codology the way you did
for blowing up reality

in grainy not-quite-blacks-or-whites
to hold on to a love I fear
to lose, or maybe never had.

The Hull Poets – And Pigeons

'...the third generation Hull poets are proving worthy
inheritors of the Larkin-Dunn estate.'
– JOHN OSBORNE ON *THE HULL POETS*, LINCOLNSHIRE &
HUMBERSIDE ARTS' *ARTS DIARY* JAN-FEB 1987.

But few of them are native to the town,
most came by chance, or maybe second choice
and some have taken off with good degrees;
others fillet fish or sign for dole.
One I know who flew the nest southwards
is honoured now, well-known and widely read
but yet unclaimed by Hull, his native town.
Such recognition isn't easily
obtained in Hull – the opportunity
might come with death: few Hullites there can be
who're unaware of Marvell's old complaint
to his coy lady, voiced by Humber's tide
above the sound of time's winged chariot;
but fewer still will know that Stevie Smith
lived here her early, valuable years.

Hull City Hall's a favoured pigeon squat
and Queen Victoria's monument is not
amused by small excretions, year on year;
by columnists and poets home to roost,
perhaps to earn, in time, the town's acclaim,
be granted all the privilege and pomp
the Three Crowns coat-of-arms would guarantee;
but clap your hands in Queen Victoria Square –
indigenous pigeons take to the air,
while alien poets are named as legatees
to Halls of Residence in Cottingham
and Bransholme's sprawling council house estates.
It matters not at all from where they came,
the pigeons or the poets; *poems* remain –
well, some – and pigeon muck accumulates.

Were I a pigeon, I'd have lost my strut,
revisiting a Humberside library,
to find my own slim volume credited
not to me, *Maurice*, but to *Margaret,*
denying me, whilst not my place of birth,
my rightful gender – hitting where it hurts –
(and Margaret's fame required no boost from me!).
And so I doubt Hull's City Fathers will
remark the passing of one *Rutherford*,
son of a Hull fish curer's manager
and writer of occasional short verse,
but should you see, one day, a chequered-blue
chance-bred streeter, in weak iambic flight,
homing on Hull like some lost poem recalled,
make room along the ledge – and let it land.

The Autumn Outings

That autumn I was quick getting away:
  only about
one-twenty on the rain-drenched Wednesday
I locked the premises and motored out,
all staff sent home, all workshop plant closed down,
all sense of any kind of business gone,
and not until I'd driven fifteen miles
along fast-flooding roads back into town,
past rival complexes just clinging on,
did rain let up and vision clear: those files

I'd never see again; that desk, the phone
  that shrilled all day
when first it was installed; not hear the moan
compressors made, be soothed by lathes, nor say
'Good morning George, alright?', or 'Nice one, Bert',
the human touch, no more, not to distract
them too long from their work, but just enough
to let them see I cared, and not to hurt
old feelings as I tried to breast the fact
of cancelled orders, creditors turned rough.

The friendly bank soon bared its teeth – drew blood;
  and then that bane,
the Tax Man, claimed his pound. And so, the flood.
(Fine detail dims again as, too, the pain
recedes three autumns on; yet loss stays true.)
The rain comes vicious now – wipers full speed,
dipped headlights on, rear fogs – the journey seems
to lengthen every time I live it through,
involuntarily, as when the need
for sleep is scuppered by recurring dreams.

My crowd was breast-fed clichés, meal on meal:
  to pull its weight,
nose to the grindstone, shoulder to the wheel,
and, once it stepped inside the factory gate,
was wedded to its work; slapped all the time
by Newbolt's hand: *Play up, and play the game.*
Well, this sounds fine; but what about the bloke
who's anorexic, short-nosed, cannot climb
to reach the wheel, and never makes the team?
For him such wedding tales are guffs of smoke.

Again the morning paper hits the floor –
  banner headlined
PIT CLOSURES SHOCK – and umpteen thousand more
are facing broken marriages to mines.
A few, lured by that bit-of-fresh, fool's gold,
pin hopes on boarding-houses, market-stalls;
one man sits out his protest down the pit,
while lefties call for strikes with all the old
clenched-fist salutes, and aerosol the walls:
SCARGILL FOR KING and TARZAN IS A SHIT.

Their first few days of idleness will see
  in those it hits
undreamt-of traits in personality:
some will get by and others go to bits;
the strong become the weak, the weak make good
as quickly as it's said. Then, as the days
stack up to months or, as in my case, years,
high principles get trampled in the mud
where guile and self-survival point new ways
to quick back-pocket jobs, fiddles and fears

of being caught. But fears will yield, in time,
  a sort of pride,
though not the social pride that saw men climb
from old-world swamps: a sense that one's defied
the odds, the system; finger-licked the crème,
nose-thumbed some top brass, bested those who made
the rules and all the running. What survives?
Of Us: too early yet to tell. Of Them:
'Indifferents and Incapables'; their trade
in UB40s and P45s.

In brass-lined boardrooms up and down the land
  deep in regret
a million more redundancies get planned,
while chairmen's hiked-up salaries are set,
and Urban Councils chase arrears in rents.
Wide-boys, insider-dealers, some M.P.s
grow richer by a second home in Spain,
a custom-plated white Mercedes Benz,
that new portfolio. True-blue disease.
The spores of loss, somewhere becoming gain.

October, 1992

View from Hessle Road

(For Jean Hartley)

Old Bikeclips with the size 12 Oxfords wrote,
but eloquently, of a *cut-price crowd*.
I'm here to argue on a moral note
not that his choice of phrase be disallowed,
but that perhaps there's something to be learned
in asking why it was he wrote of them,
not they of him. Supposing that we turned
the *flat-faced trolley* round for once; what then?
Let's say we told those *grim* and *head-scarved wives*
from fishy-smelling streets that they were owed
a swipe at Hull's late bard: 'Oozee?' perhaps
they'd gob out from *the side of their own lives*.
'We've never 'eard of 'im down 'Ezzle Road.
No, bollocks. Poetsarra....crowdacraps!'

Three Poems by David Wheatley

At the Sign of Ye Olde White Hart

'every man can dig water at his door; and they cannot
bury a corpse there but the grave first drowns him ere it
burys him'
– THE LIFE OF MASTER JOHN SHAWE

Dead men in a city besieged,
your own graves would harry you out.
The pavement eel's stone slither
along the old town's dark intestine
shows where they follow
their shadows to spawn. One
passageway leads to another,
one courtyard swallows another,
until all passageways are one
and every dead-end turns
like a folded paper trick
inside out. Do not expect spice
from the Land of Green Ginger,
though there is powder aplenty.
A sworn rite governs our fellowship
and only my skull in a box besides
be privy: the potboy crouched
by the smallest window in England
awaits but the signal. Small
acts of sedition multiply:
chalk marks on the pavement
cry death and the misericord
under your bottom has started
to flap in the breeze. The city
gates stay shut, let his Majestie
make of this what he maye;

the skull has spoken. The shadows
spawn and crawl into the shadows
to die. *How you have bled
for me, o my Kingdome.*
The Land of Green Ginger
turns itself inside out
to a dream of green fields:
*yet may we attain to that place
of peace in our hearts.* There is
no way out and we leave tonight.

Drypool in Old Photographs

1

The man on the corner repeats
at intervals down the street,
as though in a trick photographer's

loop: hands on hips, in fob
pockets, ignoring the see-through dog
ghosting along the pub wall

behind him feeding on air,
on the ghost of a promise
of gristle and bone.

2

Dawn in the brewery yard
finds ice on the dung,
the drayhorse's breath

steaming into the lens.
The barrels tumble chiming
into riverside cellars

and are sprung in a week;
the drayman's further-off
judgement day promises

the bump and jolt of a cemetery
clearance and only then
the vile dust settled at last.

3

The dog and I fall into step.
Peer through his vitreous ribs
and watch the brickwork rewind,

decade on decade. Does he
want feeding? There aren't
shadows enough to sate him.

Sharp against my ribs too,
the ghost of a torn-down future
pushes, prods, and will out.

The Lock-Keeper's Daughter

Take me away from this terrible place,
very slowly, by barge, rising through
the frothy lock outside my window
like an old cinema organ.
Ours will have been the most tacit
of courtships, the most offhand
of consummations as I step
aboard from the vegetable patch.
Expressionless townsfolk will process
from the church to the water's edge
and my discarded bouquet float by
to a wheeze of an accordeon waltz.
I too have dreamed of a tattooed
first mate and an infestation
of cats in the saucepans and hold.
The candour of my wedding dress
will face down scarecrows
and cornfields from the prow.
Take me away from this terrible place
two or three miles down the water,
no more: nowhere else can I
be happy but where the water voles
splash and the kingfisher combusts.
I hear the lock close behind me
and grant the water its steely
abolition of our having
ever passed through. I will walk
the length of the barge backwards
to you and into our future.

Three Poems by Susan Wicks

Nuclear

Each morning as I round the bend,
the same shock –
that flash of river light, the bridge,
the cooling-towers –
always that first sight gasp
as if they've been dropped there –

Yet the landscape knows them: a fragment of old stone
moves sideways, and through a tangle of red
the river glitters, the bridge
spins out its turquoise cobweb and there they stand
like a cruet – squat on the flood-plain, lit
apricot, steaming quietly into this end of night.

I've heard there's a place where fish
swim up and down a ladder, mouthing through murk
like cruising angels;
where a student strung himself up for days
from a concrete cliff while the canal
sent back his image;
where they hand out packages of pills
to every household, in case of leaks.

But here at my open window the field's
rippled with leaves, and blue,
the every morning noise
of cock-crow, unidentified shadows finger-flapping across.

Cycling to See the Fish-Ladder

Do they riffle their translucent fins
between the rungs to inch up?
Or do they effortlessly rise
as if through someone's sleep
to do what people do
with ladders – search and replace
a frost-cracked tile, or shake a tree
into a waiting skirt? Each trunk I pedal past
swells and shrills with cicadas before it fades.

But when, blinded by sweat, I finally arrive
the ladder's shut
by a Red Alert. *Merci
de votre compréhension.* I straddle my bike
and read what power means
to fish and spawning-grounds. I think I understand:
a glitch and the dream floats belly-up,
the waters of the Garonne
log-jammed and stinking. There's only the sky's

unbroken blue, the tree's small pool of shadow,
a woman's leaning bike. Nothing you can pull out
in a shining shaft, no wooden feet
to dent the mud,
no uprights you can steady against death.

Pistachios

A darkening January afternoon.
I stand at the kitchen window absently eating
pistachios left over from Christmas; outside, a blur
of hydrangea as I slide
the edge of my nail between the curved wings of a shell.
They say sex is a kind of dying.

At a certain time of life –
you never know exactly when
or where or how fast – sex leaves.
It's like a tide
slowly leaving a beach, imperceptibly exposing
rocks like bony fingers, hidden tongues of sand
and sometimes the rank on improbable rank
of mussels close as bristles –
millions of them, blue-black,
crowding the surface – like the teeth of combs
or petrified fur
that teases the soles of your bare feet
raw – a whole glittering expanse
of blue-black points, and, hidden inside,
that throb of flesh. As the tide recedes
a million brittle mouths lean shut.

A skeleton hydrangea bowls across the dusk,
shivers. I crack another shell open,
feeling saliva spurt
at the green thought
of pistachios, salt on my lips, shells light as paper.

Contributors

Peter Didsbury was born in Lancashire and moved to Hull as a child. He returned to Hull after reading English and Hebrew at Oxford University. His latest publication is *Scenes from a Long Sleep: New and Collected Poems* (Bloodaxe Books, 2003). His work appears in *A Rumoured City*.

Douglas Dunn, editor of *A Rumoured City* and several other anthologies, was born in Renfrewshire, Scotland. He is the author of short stories and plays, besides numerous collections of poetry, the first of which was *Terry Street* (1969) and the most recent, *New and Selected Poems: 1964-2000* (Faber, 2003). He was awarded the OBE in 2003.

Andy Fletcher was born in Halifax, and now lives in Hull. His poems have appeared in such magazines as *bête noir*, *Tears in the Fence, Outlaw* and *Fire*. His collection, *The Mile Long Piano,* appeared from Ragged Raven Press in 2007.

Tony Flynn, whose poems appear in *A Rumoured City,* has published three full-length collections, *A Strange Routine* and *Body Politic* from Bloodaxe Books, and *The Mermaid Chair – New and Selected Poems,* from Dream Catcher Books, 2008. His work has appeared widely in magazines and anthologies. 'Seeing Voices' won first prize in the English Association Fellows' Poetry Prize Competition in 2007. He is employed full-time in Brighton where he leads a small team of social workers and psychologists working in the field of child protection.

Cliff Forshaw teaches in the English Department at Hull University. His most recent full-length collection of poems is *Trans* (The Collective Press, Wales, 2005). His chapbook *Wake* was joint-winner of the Flarestack Pamplet Competition, 2009.

Sam Gardiner was born in Northern Ireland, but has lived in Grimsby and Cleethorpes for many years. He won the National Poetry Competition in 1993 and was nominated for a Forward Prize in 2008 His most recent collections are *Protestant Windows* (2000) and *The Night Ships* (Lagan Press, 2007).

Chris Greenhalgh graduated from the University of Hull in 1984. After living and working in Italy and Athens for five years, he returned to Hull to complete a PhD on the poet Frank O'Hara. He received a Gregory Award for his own poetry in 1992, and has since published three volumes with Bloodaxe: *Stealing the Mona Lisa* (1994), *Of Love, Death & the Sea-Squirt* (2000) and *The Invention of Zero* (2007). He has also published a novel, *Coco & Igor* (Headline 2002), for which he has written a screenplay. *Coco Chanel & Igor Stravinsky* closed the Cannes Film Festival in May 2009 and is due for international release in 2010. He lives and works in Kent, where he is currently Deputy Head of Sevenoaks School.

Ian Gregson's latest book of poems is *How We Met* (Salt, 2008).He has published five critical books on postwar literature and is currently writing one on Mary Oliver.He teaches in the English department at Bangor University. His poems appear in *A Rumoured City*.

T.F. Griffin has a long association with the Hull poetry scene. His poems appear in *A Rumoured City,* and he has since published several full-length collections, including *Kavita* (Shoestring Press, 2003) and *The Leveller* (Flux Gallery Press, 2006). A festschrift for his 60th birthday, *Born into an Unquiet*, edited by Ian Parks, was published by Flux Gallery Press in 2009.

Douglas Houston was born in Cardiff, grew up in Scotland and Surrey and gained his Ph.D from Hull University for research into 20th Century Poetry. Perhaps the most widely acclaimed of his poetry collections, *The Welsh Book of the Dead* was published by Seren in 2003.

Margot K. Juby's appearances in print have included *Tribune, The Scotsman, Bête Noire, The Rialto, The Wide Skirt* and *Iron.* She is the only 'new poet from Hull' (Bloodaxe, 1982) who was also a 'writer of East Anglia' (Secker and Warburg, 1977). She has published five small press collections: *Femme Fatale, Pandora's Box, Grey, The Tactful Foetus* and *Erl-King's Bride.* The first three of these publications were collected in *Triple Whammy* (Braquemard, 1996). For several years now Margot has taken no part in the tomfoolery of poetry. She prefers to spend her time in revisionist research into the life of Gilles de Rais, who was re-tried and acquitted in 1992.

David Kennedy has published three collections with Salt. Recent poetry includes the sequences _MY Atrocity_ (Oystercatcher Press, 2009) and _Mistral_ (Rack Press, 2010). He wishes to thank Glenn Storhaug for help with the translations of the repeated phrase in 'The Hull Emigration Platform'.

Angela Leighton taught for many years in the English department at the University of Hull, and is now Senior Research Fellow at Trinity College, Cambridge. She is the author of a number of critical books, including *On Form: Poetry, Aestheticism, and the Legacy of a Word* (OUP, 2007), and of two volumes of poetry, *A Cold Spell* (2000) and *Sea Level* (2007), both with Shoestring. She is currently preparing a third volume, and researching a book on the music of poetry.

Frances Leviston was born in Edinburgh in 1982, and grew up in Sheffield. She read English at St Hilda's College, Oxford, where she won the Lord Alfred Douglas Prize for Poetry in 2003. She has an MA in Writing from Sheffield Hallam University. Her pamphlet *Lighter* (Mews Press, 2004) was selected as the PBS Bulletin Pamphlet Choice for Spring 2005, and her poems have appeared in the *Times*, the *TLS*, British Council/Granta *New Writing 14*, *Poetry London* and *Poetry Review*. She received an Eric Gregory Award from the Society of Authors in 2006. Her first collection, *Public Dream*, was published in 2007 by Picador. She has worked as a librarian and a snowboarding instructor, and regularly reviews poetry for the *Guardian*. She came to Hull in 2009-2010 to lead the Fifth Quarter Poetry Workshops at Artlink Centre for Community Arts on Princes Avenue.

Roger McGough was born in Liverpool and educated at the University of Hull. A much-loved performer and poet, he has written many collections for both adults and children, including *Summer with Monika* (1967), *Out of Sequence* (1972), *Sporting Relations* (1974), *Defying Gravity* (1993), *The Way Things Are* (1999), *Everyday Eclipses* (2002) and *That Awkward Age* (2009). He now presents the BBC Radio 4 programme Poetry Please and records voice-overs for commercials. He was awarded the CBE in June 2004.

Andrew Motion was Poet Laureate from 1999 to 2009, and is Professor of Creative Writing at Royal Holloway College, University of London. He worked as a lecturer in the English Department of the University from Hull from 1976 until 1980, and it was during this time that he met Philip Larkin, whose authorised biography he later wrote.

Grace Nichols was born and educated in Guyana, and moved to Britain in 1977. She has written poetry collections for adults and children, and she is among the poets whose work is studied on the current GCSE syllabus. Her most recent collection is *Picasso, I Want my Face Back* (Bloodaxe Books, 2009) and her *Selected Poems* is due from Bloodaxe in 2010.

Sean O'Brien, Professor of Creative Writing at Newcastle University, has won a number of prizes for his poetry. He has published six collections, the most recent of which is *The Drowned Book* (Picador, 2007). A verse translation of Dante's *Inferno* was published in 2006. He grew up in Hull and some of his early poems appear in *A Rumoured City*.

Ian Parks was Writer in Residence at North Riding College, Scarborough, from 1986-1991. He won a travelling fellowship to the USA in 1994, and he was one of the National Poetry Society's designated 'New Poets' of 1996. His full-length collections include *Shell Island* (Waywiser Press) and *The Cage* (Flux Gallery Press, 2008).

Tom Paulin, poet, critic, playwright, editor and broadcaster, was born in Leeds and grew up in Belfast. His publications include *Writing to the Moment: Selected Critical Essays 1980-1996* (Faber, 1996), *The Road to Inver: Translations, Versions and Imitations 1975-2003* (Faber, 2004) and *The Secret Life of Poems* (Faber, 2007).

Tony Petch graduated in Forestry from the University of Edinburgh. He later trained as a social worker. His collection, *Vanishing Point*, is published by Ragged Raven Press.

Genny Rahtz was born in Bristol and graduated from Hull University in 1973. She has recently moved from York to Oxford where she works as an Alexander teacher. Her new collection, *Sky Burtial,* is forthcoming from Flux Gallery Press.

Frank Redpath (1927-1990) was born in Hull, and after spending some years in London as a writer for children's comics, returned to Hull where he taught at the College of Further Education. His first collection of Poems was *In The Village* (Sonus, 1986). He was preparing a second collection when he died. *The Rialto* subsequently published this collection in 1996 as *How it Turned Out,* with an introduction by Sean O'Brien.

Christopher Reid has published a number of award-winning poetry collections. His most recent, *A Scattering* (Areté. 2009), was shortlisted for the Forward prize and won the Costa prize. He was the Director of the Philip Larkin Centre, University of Hull, 2008-9.

Caitríona O'Reilly was born in Dublin, and educated at Trinity College, where she completed her doctoral thesis on American literature. She has taught briefly at Hull University and currently edits *Poetry Ireland*. She has published two collections, *The Nowhere Birds* (Bloodaxe, 2001) which won the Rooney Prize for Irish Literature, and *The Sea Cabinet* (Bloodaxe, 2006).

Carol Rumens' collections of poetry include *Blind Spots* (Seren, 2008) and *De Chirico's Threads* (Seren, 2010). She was the first Director of the Philip Larkin Centre (2005-6) and is currently Visiting Professor of Creative Writing at the University of Hull.

Maurice Rutherford, born in Hull in 1922, has spent his working life as a technical writer in the ship-repairing industry on both banks of the Humber. He has published three collections of poetry: *Slipping the Tugs* (Lincolnshire & Humberside Arts, 1982), *This Day Dawning* (Peterloo Poets, 1989) and *Love is a Four-Letter World* (Peterloo Poets, 1994) and a pamphlet *After the Parade* (Shoestring Press, 1996). His *New and Selected Poems* will be published by Shoestring Press in 2011.

David Wheatley was born in Dublin in 1970 and has lived in Hull since 2000. His poetry collections, all published by Gallery Press, are: *Thirst* (1997), *Misery Hill* (2000), and *Mocker* (2006). He has also edited the work of James Clarence Mangan for Gallery Press and Samuel Beckett's *Selected Poems 1930-1989* for Faber and Faber.

Susan Wicks's first book of poems, *Singing Underwater* (Faber, 1992), won the Aldeburgh Poetry Festival Prize. Since then she has published four other collections of poetry, a collection of stories, two novels and a short memoir, *Driving My Father. The Clever Daughter* (1996) was a Poetry Book Society Choice and shortlisted for both Forward and T.S. Eliot Prizes. Her most recent book of poems, *De-iced*, came out from Bloodaxe in 2007 and *Cold Spring in Winter*, her translations of the

French poet Valerie Rouzeau, in June 2009. A new collection is due from Bloodaxe in 2011. The University of Hull, where she dropped out first time round and began again in 1967, was her first real encounter with poetry: it was there she learned to analyse unaided a single short lyric by Valéry, Apollinaire or Eluard for the space of an hour under the terrifying yet not unkind eyes of Professor Garnet Rees.

Acknowledgements

Peter Didsbury's 'A Fire Shared' was first published in *Poetry Ireland Review*. 'Owl and Miner' and 'Coasts of Africa 1850' appear in *Scenes from a Long Sleep. New and Collected Poems*, Bloodaxe, 2003.

'Ripe Bananas' and 'The House of the Blind' are published here for the first time, copyright Douglas Dunn.

Andy Fletcher's 'The Boating Trip', 'The Den' and 'Meeting You' appear in *The Mile Long Piano* (Ragged Raven, 2007).

Tony Flynn's 'Seeing Voices' first appeared in *Dream Catcher Magazine*; 'The Gravity of Lovelessness' in *Thumbscrew*; and 'Body Language' in *The Slab*. All three poems appear in *The Mermaid Chair – New and Selected Poems* (Dream Catcher Books, 2008).

Cliff Forshaw's 'Wake' appeared in the catalogue for *The Art of Love* exhibition at The Gallery and the Bargehouse at Oxo Tower Wharf, London, February 2005, and the chapbook *Wake* (Flarestack Poets, 2009). "Ned Kelly's Eyes" appeared online in *EnterText* 7.2 (Brunel University, 2007), and the chapbook *A Ned Kelly Hymnal* (A Paper Special Edition/Cherry on the Top Press, 2008).

Sam Gardiner's 'Second Person', 'A Ring' and 'Brick Worker' appear in *The Night Ships* (Lagan Press, 2007).

'Last Days' and 'On the Shiants' are published here for the first time, copyright Chris Greenhalgh.

T.F. Griffin's 'The Canal', 'The Climb' and 'Winter Sun' are from *Selected Poems: 1974-2008* (Flux Gallery Press, 2008).

Douglas Houston's 'Sunday on the Cuillin' appeared in *The Welsh Book of the Dead* (Seren, 2000). 'Shackleton et Fils' appeared in *The Hunters in the Snow*, (Bloodaxe, 1995) 'Your Only Man' copyright Douglas Houston.

Margot K. Juby's 'The Blood-Red Tattoo' has appeared in *Braquemard* and *Splizz*. 'Les Très Riches Heures de Gilles de Rais' was published in *Poetry Nottingham International, Sol, The Mutiny Poems*, and *Quantum Leap*. 'Crow Town' is published here for the first time, copyright Margot K. Juby.

David Kennedy's 'Arc' and 'The Hull Emigration Platform' appeared in *Architexts* (Humber Mouth City Arts, 2007).

Angela Leighton's 'Windfall' was a 'Poem of the Week' on the Guardian Online books blogs during 2008. 'Form' and 'Sortilege' are published here for the first time, copyright Angela Leighton.

Frances Leviston's 'Sight' appears in *Public Dream* (Picador, 2007, © Frances Leviston, 2007, courtesy of Pan MacMillan, London.) 'Story' was commended in the 2008 Arvon Poetry Competition.

Roger McGough's 'An Apology' and 'What does your Father do?' were originally published in *Everyday Eclipse* (Viking, 2002).

'The Korean Memorial at Hiroshima', 'Over Here' and 'The New York Planetarium' copyright Andrew Motion.

Grace Nichols's 'Outward from Hull', 'Advice on Crossing a Street in Delhi' and 'A Statement from the Empire State Building appeared in *Picasso, I Want My Face Back* (Bloodaxe Books, 2009).

Ian Parks' 'North Landing' appears in *Love Poems: 1979-2009* (Flux Gallery Press, 2009). 'Lazarus' and 'Downpour' are published here for the first time, copyright Ian Parks.

Tom Paulin's 'A Single Weather' appeared in *The Road to Inver* (Faber, 2004).'Matins' appeared in *Walking a Line* (Faber, 1994) and 'Settlers' in *A State of Justice* (Faber, year?)

Tony Petch 'Two Sonnets' and 'The Holding' are previously unpublished.

Genny Rahtz's 'Bird Prints' was published in *Prayer Flags* (Flux Gallery Press, Leeds, 2006). 'Embodied Memory' and 'Sky Windows' will appear in *Sky Burial,* also published by Flux Gallery Press, in 2010. 'Embodied Memory' will also appear in *Dream Catcher* poetry magazine in 2011.

Frank Redpath's 'Story Time' And 'How it Turned Out' appeared in *How it Turned Out* (The Rialto, 1996).

Sean O'Brien's 'Blizzard' and 'Fantasia on a Theme of James Wright' were published in *The Drowned Book,* Picador, 2007. 'The Citizens' is published here for the first time, copyright Sean O'Brien.

Caitríona O'Reilly's 'A Quartet for the Falcon' and 'Now or When' are published in *The Sea Cabinet* (Bloodaxe Books, 2006).

Christopher Reid's 'Kandy', 'Ink' and 'Chorale' are from *A Box of Tricks for Anna Zyx* (Ondt & Gracehoper, 2009). 'Chorale' was first published in *Drift*, and commissioned by the Humber Mouth Festival.

Maurice Rutherford's 'The Cod Farm', 'The Hull Poets — and Pigeons' and 'The Autumn Outings' appear in *Love is a Four-Letter Word* (Peterloo Poets, 1994) and 'View from Hessle Road' in *After the Parade* (Shoestring Press, 1996)

David Wheatley's 'Drypool in Old Photographs' appeared in *An Unofficial Roy Fisher* (Ed. Peter Robinson, Shearsman, 2010). 'The Lock-Keeper's Daughter' and 'At the Sign of Ye Olde White Hart' copyright David Wheatley.

'Nuclear' and 'Cycling to See the Fish Ladder' copyright Susan Wicks. 'Pistachios' appears in *Women's Work* (Eds. Eva Salzman and Amy Wack, Seren, 2008) and was first published in *Poetry London*; 'Nuclear' was first published in the *London Review of Books*; 'Cycling to See the Fish-ladder' in *Poetry Review*.

Philip Larkin Society

Old City, New Rumours is published with the assistance of the Philip Larkin Society (www.philiplarkin.com) as part of the commemoration of the 25th anniversary of the death of Philip Larkin (www.larkin25.co.uk).

Volumes in the Philip Larkin Society Monograph Series

A.T. Tolley, *Larkin at Work: A study of Larkin's mode of composition as seen in his Workbooks*, University of Hull Press, 1997

Richard Palmer and John White (eds), *Larkin's Jazz: Essays and Reviews 1940-84*, Continuum, 2001 (originally published as *Reference Back*, University of Hull Press, 1999)

Maeve Brennan, *The Philip Larkin I Knew*, Manchester University Press, 2002